TO HAVE
AND
TO HOLD

A FRESH LOOK AT PHONES & MARRIAGE
AND HOW TO WIN AT BOTH

DOUG FIELDS

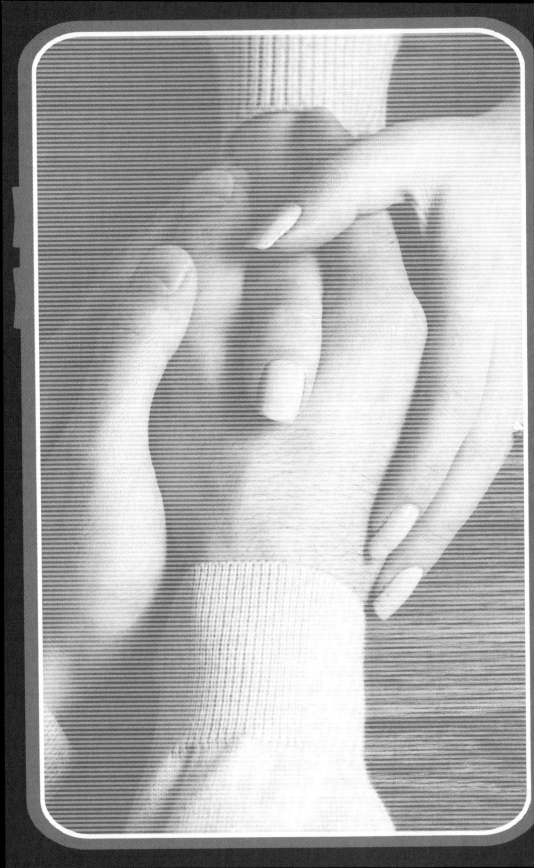

Dedication

Cathy Fields: For 35 years, I've marveled at your beauty, love, faith, and passion. Thank you for loving me so well and modeling the power of presence.

• • •

THANKS

I'm extremely grateful to my friend and brilliant designer Jason Pearson for hearing my speech on phones and marriage and saying, "That would make a great book!" Thanks for planting the seed to write this, as well as for your creativity in designing this book. You're the best! I'm also very grateful to a team of friends who read the manuscript and offered their pearls of wisdom: Seth Bartlette, Josh Griffin, Megan Hutchinson, John Keim, Ronald Long, Amanda Maguire, Misha McGill, Ivy McBirney, Jeff Selph, Anthony Taylor, Derry Prenkert, Tim Wildsmith, and Allison Williams. Special thanks to Drew Tilton and Josh Pease for helping me know what to capitalize and where commas should go and editing my inappropriate humor. And to my dear friend, Fadi Cheikha, for providing me with a great office and an endless supply of high-quality licorice.

INTRODUCTION

I love my wife.

I love my kids.

I love my friends.

I even love most of the people I work with.

I love corn on the cob, anything with caramel, Swedish fish, CrossFit, hot showers, and comedies—as I really love to laugh.

I also love my phone! Seriously, I *really* love my phone.

Like you, I love a lot of different things. I can easily use the word "love" when describing different types of affections, and yet they don't all have the same level of importance in my life. You get that … it's most likely the same with you.

Yet, when I'm not paying attention, I can find my love and affection drifting toward misguided targets. As a result, I miss out on amazing opportunities to love the one (my wife) whom I'm supposed to love more than anyone in the entire world.

Over the last few years, I've encountered many couples at my speaking engagements who point to their phone-affection as a primary source of tension in their relationship. This shouldn't be a surprise, as the "new normal" is couples (primarily at restaurants) sitting knee-to-knee, but no longer eye-to-eye—instead, with heads down, staring into a compelling screen. Phones have become a relational distraction.

I wrote this short book because I really believe some small, simple, doable changes can strengthen a marriage while weakening the power of your phone. I believe this because I've personally made these changes.

I promise you these changes won't require you to ditch your phone or give up on technology. As I mentioned, I love my phone—it's a constant companion. But, at times, it was also my mobile mistress. It's a small (4-ounce), seductive device, unparalleled in its ability to deliver entertainment, information, and distraction. (I really do love it.)

But I want to love people more!

And, I want to have a great marriage!

So, with full admission of my own guilty phone behavior and a no-shame approach toward yours, I want to help you develop a healthier marriage. You have what it takes. Actually, your phone habits have been teaching you how to love your spouse in stronger ways. While I don't want to get too far ahead of myself, let me just hint that some of the actions you've been taking with your phone are the types of actions your marriage needs. I'll leave it at that—you've got to read the rest.

Speaking of reading … uh, well … if you're more of a phone person than a reader, don't worry. This is a quick, fun read. As you'll soon see, it's designed with a bunch of pictures so you might accidentally forget that you're reading and begin to think you're still on Instagram (I've got your back). Actually, your short investment of time may be just what you need to enhance your love and strengthen your marriage.

In a world where phones make it so easy to be connected, the pages ahead will help you avoid becoming disconnected from the person you love the most.

Ready? Let's do this!

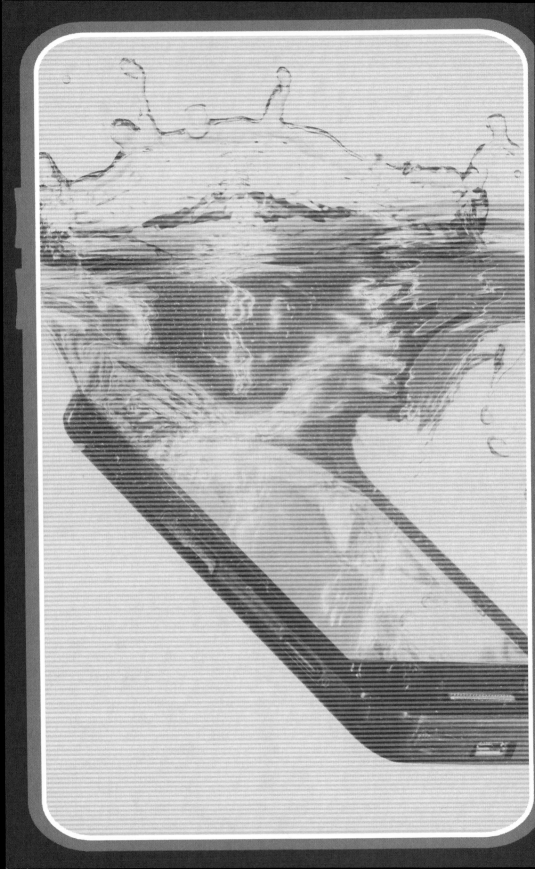

HOME SCREEN

CHAPTER ONE

There have been some incredibly helpful inventions in the past century (i.e., the telephone, the internet, the child leash).

Not long ago, "pain management" during a trip to the dentist involved guzzling whiskey and biting down on a belt, but then local anesthesia was invented. Trips that used to take weeks and (per my experience playing the game Oregon Trail) involved death from diarrhea and measles and whatever dysentery is now happen in just a few hours, thanks to the Wright Brothers' discovering manned flight. Ever had someone fool you into thinking your zipper was down? Well, you have Mr. Gideon Sundback, inventor of the zipper, to thank for that. (Actually, the dumb joke isn't his fault, and the zipper is pretty handy.)

Some inventions, however, aren't quite as useful. In 1937, for instance, Jack Milford built the first-ever two-person baby slingshot. Maybe that's not what that invention was meant to be, but I look at that picture and all I imagine is an airborne infant—incoming!

Or how about the best marriage-improving invention of all time, the Double Toilet? (You may not want to turn the page.)

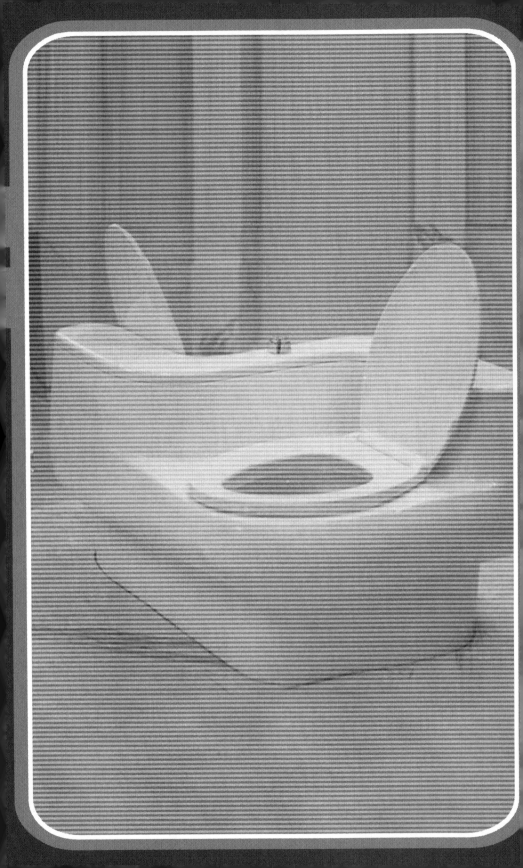

As a self-proclaimed marriage expert with decades of experience, trust me when I tell you that nothing grows marital intimacy faster than mutual bowel evacuation. It's nature's aphrodisiac. Go buy a tandem toilet today.

Seriously though, it's funny to me that someone was so convinced people would want to poop together that they put time and energy into making a prototype. I mean, someone really thought my invention* will make life easier for people, when all it did was create a new set of complications (like, for instance, your spouse never being attracted to you again).

The truth is that all inventions, even good ones, are a double-edged sword. Think about the mobile phone. When Alexander Graham Bell invented the phone in 1876, he couldn't have imagined his invention would evolve into a camera, email transmitter, road map, calendar, contact list, and our primary source of entertainment and news. We only use it for talking when absolutely forced to. On some days this amazingly powerful 4-ounce tool that remains glued to the palm of our hand is our only connection to the outside world. What an incredible invention! This must have astronomically improved the quality of our life and made us so much happier, right?

Sure, except for when it doesn't.

*I don't know if this invention has a name. If it were me I'd call it the "Double Deuce."

I recently saw a news story about a second grader assigned to write an essay on an invention he did not like. The child wrote about his mom's phone and how he wished it had never been invented. He explained: "I don't like the phone because my parents are on it all the time. A phone is sometimes a really bad habit. I hate my mom's phone and I wish she never had one."

The story made national news. Teachers from all over the country said this boy's opinion wasn't an isolated one, that many children in their classrooms feel they take second place to a parent's phone. This boy's story is heart-wrenching and, if you're like me, guilt-inducing. Dozens of times I've caught myself ignoring my family while staring at my phone ... and that's just today. I often wonder whether the amazing invention that is the mobile phone is actually having unintended impacts on my closest relationships? Is it possible that, like the Double Deuce™, phones are not as great an idea as they seem?

I have the incredible privilege of traveling around the country, talking with people about their marriages. One thing I hear regularly from frustrated spouses is that when it comes to receiving attention, they come a distant second to their husband or wife's phone. An email I recently received from one man described how his wife's addiction to a phone game was creating issues in their sex life. Her overuse and under-awareness of its impact had forged a disconnect in their relationship.

17

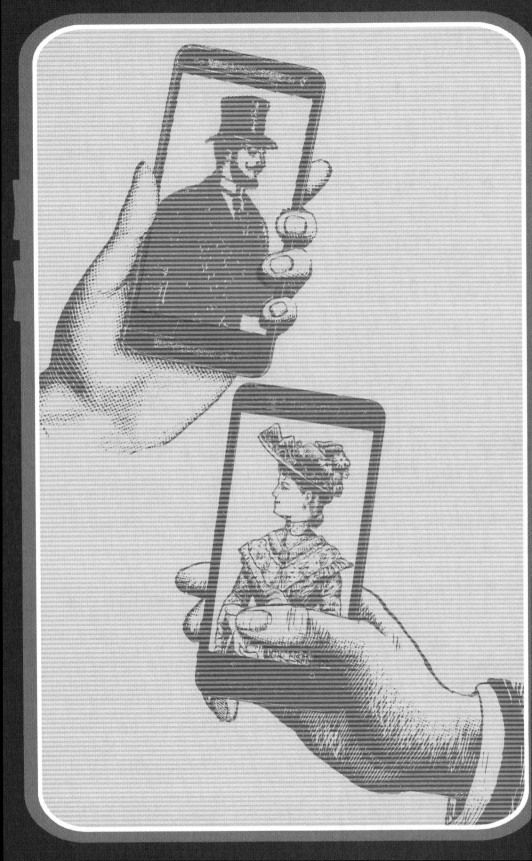

A disconnect. Think about that.

Do you see the irony there? This invention that's supposed to connect us to each other is causing disconnections. Everything in our society—from social media, to conversations, to news outlets, to entertainment—is increasingly flowing through our phones. App notifications ping and vibrate and pop up, drawing us back to our screens. The creators of the games on our phones, knowing we have access to them 24/7, create incentives for opening the app as often as possible. Researchers spend millions of dollars finding the most effective way to sell you the newest phone. These people are not wondering, "How do we help our customers cultivate rich, fulfilling relationships?" They're thinking, "How do we keep people addicted to our product?"

I'm not anti-technology. I love the perks and conveniences of phone use. I have Twitter and Instagram. I have a Facebook page I aggressively ignore. I'm not suggesting we all become Amish, avoid electricity, and roll around in buggies and bonnets (unless that's a fantasy you and your spouse are into—in which case, go for it!) Our phones provide plenty of positives. When used correctly, they can even benefit our relationships. The question isn't whether our phones are bad, but how do we leverage our phones as a source of marital connection, not disconnection?

• What are some ways you can enhance your connection with your spouse through your phone?

CHAPTER TWO

This is a tricky topic, so let's start by dialing into the immense power our phones possess.

Our phones have a power far beyond their batteries. They affect our life, our relationships, and our marriage—sometimes in positive ways.

My phone's most obvious positive marital impact is how simple it makes staying in touch with my wife, Cathy. Whether it's checking in throughout our day (we text each other a lot!) or connecting via FaceTime while I am traveling, our phones connect us in ways that weren't possible when we were newlyweds (which will be a great grandpa story to tell my grandchildren someday. "Back when Grandma and I got married, we didn't even have mobile phones!")

My phone makes it super easy to capture the fun memories of life, like a vacation in New York or us playing with our granddaughter. My phone doubles as a photo album containing thousands of pictures, and if you're ever near me, I will try to show you all of them. No doubt you'll love it.

When used well, my phone makes life massively more efficient. I can check the weather, share my calendar, get directions, check my bank account, pay for gas, hire a dog walker, or hitch a ride with a stranger who Uber promises me isn't a serial killer, all with a few taps and swipes.

Now that is power!

POWERED
UP?

What's crazy is how normal this has become. Everything our phones do is so integrated into daily existence, we forget how not so long ago something like a mobile phone would have been seen only in a sci-fi film. We just don't give this much thought.

And that's why our phones are also a problem.

We don't give them much thought.

Have you ever seen one of those news stories about a person in Florida (why is it always Florida?) who was attacked by a dangerous animal they kept as a pet? I always wonder what the person with the 18-foot man-eating pet python was thinking. Can't they see that "man-eating" is right there in the python's name? This is the danger of routine though, right? You can have something immensely powerful and potentially dangerous right by your side, but over time you get used to it.

You become inoculated to the danger.

You let your guard down and become careless.

Now think about your phone. No, seriously, get it out and stare at it

for a second. Looks harmless, right? It's been aesthetically designed to feel comforting, friendly, and accessible.

It's got colorful apps and eye-catching red notifications you'll spend all day trying to get rid of, only to see more pop up in a different app later. It makes pleasant dings and plays musical numbers to let you know people want to connect with you!

It fits in your pocket. It's a friend! And yet this "friend" leaves you one tap away from some of the most harmful content human depravity has ever imagined. It's a screen we lose ourselves in as we try to escape the underlying anxiety in our lives. We compulsively check the same social media platform we just refreshed 30 seconds ago, in search of a distraction. As much as we'd like to deny its power, phone addiction is a real thing!

CHAPTER THREE

In marriage, there is no shortage of hazards and distractions. Financial stress, communication issues, kids, lack of kids, too many kids, which way the toilet paper roll is meant to face (there are two people on this earth: those who drop toilet paper over the front, and sociopaths) ... all these factors contribute to marital tension. Marriages are filled with so many Giant Adult-Sized Complications it's easy to think our phone is just a minor nuisance, not a marriage-wrecker. But research is increasingly clear that our phones are an 18-foot python, and it's sleeping next to us at night.

Family law experts report a steady increase in separated couples who cite the misuse of phones and social media during divorce proceedings. They use the term "Technology Interference" as a fancy legal way of saying, "I'm tired of my partner looking at their screen instead of me."

Why is this such a big deal? How can so many couples allow these pocket computers to get between them? Therapists would say phone use is not generally the direct cause of divorce. Rather, phones place pressure on the pre-existing fault lines in a relationship, turning them into cataclysmic earthquakes. If a wife already believes she is unwanted, she will perceive excessive phone use as rejection. If a husband already feels his spouse is emotionally distant, each phone glance confirms "she wants to be anywhere but with me."

We live in a world where everything has a clever label, and there's a term for this, too: it's called phubbing, a combination of the words phone and snubbing. Phubbing is defined as "the act of snubbing someone by looking at your phone instead of paying attention to them."

An article in TIME Health stated that "several studies have shown that phubbing makes face-to-face interactions less meaningful." It went on to say that those who phubbed or were being phubbed (I know that sounds weird) found relationships, conversations, even food less enjoyable. Think about that. Your phone has the power to suck the flavor out of your food.

The American Psychological Association calls this phenomenon "technoference." It is defined as "the interference of technology in our relationships." In one study, researchers found that "participants who rated more technoference in their relationships also reported more conflict over technology use, lower relationship satisfaction, more depressive symptoms, and lower life satisfaction."

Are you starting to get the picture? Your phone might not be bad, but it is dangerous. This amazing and powerful invention can make you depressed, dampen your senses, and wreck your marriage. There's a reason why the Twilight Zone-esque Netflix show Black Mirror is so popular. Somewhere, deep in our souls, we know our relationship with technology is near-nightmarish.

So what does all this mean?

Healthy marriages are mindful of the power they give their phones.

Go back and read that sentence again. And then return to answer the following questions:

• What's the one thing I do with my phone that gets on my spouse's nerves?

• Think about a time you felt phubbed by your spouse. How did it make you feel?

• When is a time when you're most likely to phub someone?

• On a scale of 1–10, how much of a problem do you think your phone is?

NO PROBLEMS
WHATSOEVER   ADDICTION
(1) (2) (3) (4) (5) (6) (7) (8) (9) (10)

• On a scale of 1–10, how might others describe your phone use?

IT'S NEVER
AN ISSUE   INTERVENTION
(1) (2) (3) (4) (5) (6) (7) (8) (9) (10)

Take the FREE phone addiction test:
https://virtual-addiction.com/smartphone-compulsion-test/

Right now you might be thinking, "Okay, Doug. Great! You've made me feel sufficiently guilty/terrified, but how do I actually do something about this?"

Well, the first step is to take a page from the Alcoholics Anonymous playbook and admit we have a problem.

CHAPTER FOUR

NOMOPHOBIA

No. 1 | WE **OBSESS** OVER OUR PHONE

Statistics say Americans check their phone on average every six minutes they are awake. That's 150 times each day. Imagine if you saw someone compulsively perform a task—like checking to see if the door is locked, or untying and retying their shoes—150 times a day. You would be concerned. That's not healthy behavior!

Because phone addiction is so common, we normalize and justify our addictive behavior. But have you ever wondered why you panic when you reach for your phone and it's not there? The American Psychological Association has given this fear a name: "nomophobia" (as in, "fear of no mobile"). Apparently, this specific fear affects over 50 percent of the population. In contrast, only 38 percent of people say they're fearful of a loved one dying, which means the fear of losing a phone is greater than the fear of losing a family member!*

In a recent survey, 72 percent of people reported spending most of their lives within five feet of their phones. Sixty-six percent sleep next to their phone. Twenty percent would rather go shoeless for a week than temporarily release their phone from their presence. Seventy percent of women and 61 percent of men describe feeling separation anxiety when they are away from their phones. If that is not addiction, then I don't know what is.

*"How's Grandpa feeling?" becomes "Where's my phone?"

39

Ugh. Addiction. That's an ugly word, right?

When thinking of addiction, we normally think of alcohol, gambling, and pornography (a.k.a. a normal weekend trip to Las Vegas). We see addiction as tragic, life-wrecking, and horrifying. So when I say we're addicted to our phones, you might feel defensive. "No, I'm not," you might think. "I just really like having my phone nearby. What's the big deal?"

The big deal is that addicts make lousy spouses.

If we're not willing to label our phone addiction, we won't have honest conversations with ourselves (and our spouses) about it. We won't create space to hear our spouse say, "This could be hurting our marriage."

No. 2 | WE **TOUCH** OUR PHONE CONSTANTLY

Not only do we swipe and double-tap our phones, but we also fondle and caress them. We feel a sense of power or comfort having them in our grasp.

Have you noticed how phones migrated from our pockets and purses to a constant hand companion? Mindless scrolling, swiping, liking, and texting means our phones are constantly in our palms, and since this is sometimes cumbersome, we've turned them into watches so we don't have to worry about dropping them. In fact, people are so glued to their phones that, in 2018, New Jersey approved a new texting law. If you are caught texting while walking, it's going to cost you an $85 fine (yet another reason not to live in Jersey).

Our constant phone touching and holding is creating new medical conditions connected to our grip. Popular Science reports, "Using a phone or tablet causes symptoms that look a lot like carpal tunnel syndrome." The author wrote: "We hope this study will raise awareness among electronic device users of the importance of postural variations during their use and … the need for rest periods to avoid prolonged use."

"Postural variations" isn't a sex tip, but it is a pretty wild takeaway: we are touching our phones so much it's physically hurting us.

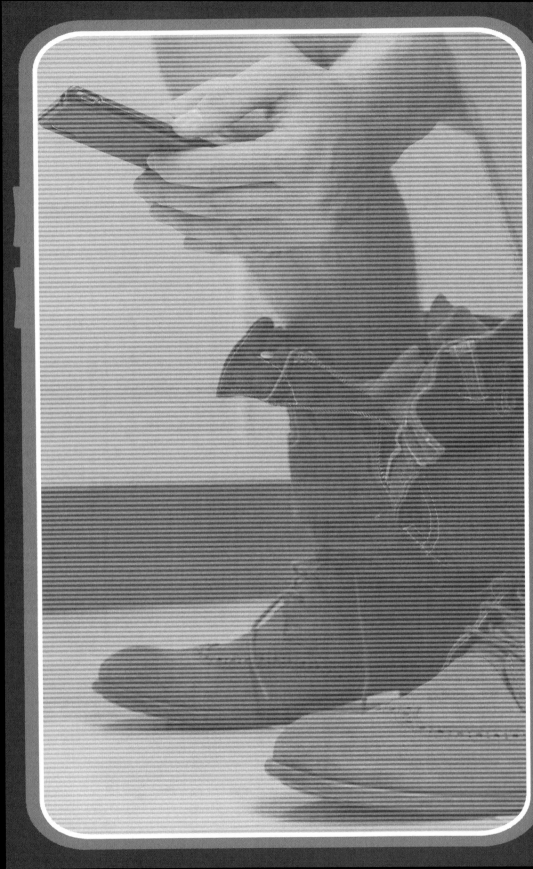

No. 3 | WE TAKE OUR PHONE TO **PRIVATE LOCATIONS**

There's a 75 percent chance if I "like" one of your Instagram photos, I'm sitting on the toilet*. This is another reason why the Double Deuce™ is a bad idea—you'd just be jointly ignoring each other, staring at pictures of your friend's trip to Italy.

Surprisingly, the toilet isn't the only private place we take our phones.

I was reading an article on phone obsession that said "6 percent of British [people] admit to texting or answering a call during sex." (There's probably a "setting your phone to vibrate" joke here, but I am far too dignified to make it.) Ha! Crazy British people, right? Well 9 percent of American adults admit to the exact same thing. Thirty-three percent of adults regularly check their phones during a dinner date, and honestly, that number feels low to me.

We've all lost track of the number of times we've seen couples sitting together for a meal, knee to knee, but no longer eye to eye. Both have their gaze focused on the little screen in their hand, seeking connection and approval from the internet rather than the person most suited to give it to them.

Or what about other non-physical, intimate moments with your spouse? How often do our phones interrupt our one-on-one conversations? Our phones constantly compete for our affection and attention. Couples can't experience intimate moments if they're constantly distracted by the power of the phone. And when you're obsessed, there is no private moment your phone won't invade.

*Sorry, not sorry.

45

No. 4 | WE MAKE SURE OUR PHONE IS **TURNED ON** & **CHARGED**

The famous moral philosopher Jerry Seinfeld has a comedy routine about our phone's battery running parallel to our own energy level. He says, "Have you ever noticed when your phone is at 14 percent you actually begin to give up on life?" It seems funny, but did you know there is actually something called "low-battery anxiety"? Apparently, 90 percent of phone users panic when they are losing power on their phones.

To avoid the panic, we work tirelessly to make sure our phone stays charged. We buy chargers and portable power banks, and, if necessary, we'll switch to low-power mode. I've even seen a small solar panel attached to a backpack just to ensure the user never ran low.

We all know by experience that it's all fun and games until our phone battery gets low. Then life gets serious.

No. 5 | WE SPEND **MONEY** ON OUR PHONE

Since the iPhone's release in 2007, the average iPhone user is estimated to have spent $20,000 to $30,000 on phones and phone-related expenses. That's a down payment on a house in some areas of the country (or half a semester of your kid's college tuition).

Buying the newest model of phone, getting the premium version of that app, the best Bluetooth devices, protective cases, cracked-screen repair kits, and phone chargers together make up a multi-billion dollar industry. And that doesn't take into account the money you spend keeping the thing working. It is estimated that in 2017, AT&T made $26 billion in revenue from providing cellular service alone. No matter what you believe about your phone, it certainly isn't cheap.

No. 6 | WE GIVE OUR PHONE ATTENTION **FIRST THING** IN THE MORNING

What do the first few moments of your day look like? If you're like most people, you grab your phone while you're still in bed to check your email or Instagram feed or stocks (to see if Apple or Google are falling because of this book). All too often, our phone captures our first thoughts of the day.

This early morning attention is largely due to one factor: we sleep next to it! A large percentage of people go to bed each night with their phones within arm's reach. When asked why, most reply with: "It's my alarm clock."

About that. Um … people know traditional alarm clocks exist, right? Let me assure you that after a brief internet search (from my phone), I discovered several selections of clocks on Amazon, all of which could help you wake up. And if you tend to be too much of a snooze button-aholic, there's even an alarm clock that simulates the light of sunrise.

My point is that we've enmeshed our phones into our lives at such a deep level we've forgotten we have options. I was recently talking to a couple that banned all technology from their bedroom. Period. And honestly, my first thought was, "Well, I could never do that." But of course I could! It would be a bit of a sacrifice at first, but wouldn't having a healthier marriage be worth it?

51

No. 7 | WE **MAKE MEMORIES** WITH OUR PHONE

In the last seven years, 250 people have died while taking selfies. So obsessed with documenting life via social media that they lost track of where they actually were, and literally ended their lives. That's obsession. For some, not a moment can pass without snapping a pic and posting it on Instagram, Snapchat, or the social media platforms invented while you read this that I am way too old to ever understand. An entire social media industry has been built on us manufacturing memories to show other people, and we've conditioned ourselves to care more about that than the memories themselves! Instead of making memories worth repeating, we're creating a digital archive of our lives.

• • •

These seven points aren't exhaustive, but they're enough to drive home how ever-present our phones are, and how oddly affectionate we are toward them. Look back at that list and notice how it uses words like "obsessing," "touching," "making memories," and "private locations." Don't those sound intimate? Almost … like … you know … activities we should be sharing with our spouses … (see where I'm going here?)

Think about it. What if you treated your spouse like you treat your phone? I don't mean poking and swiping them (again, unless you're both into that and have a safe word), but taking the time and energy we pour into our phones and redirecting those resources for the benefit of our spouse.

CHAPTER FIVE

Let's look at the 7 actions we just mentioned,
but with a marriage twist.

No. 1 | OBSESS OVER YOUR ~~PHONE~~ SPOUSE

I'm obviously referring to a healthy obsession, a fascination, a sense of being captivated by your spouse.

I know that when Cathy is thinking about me, cheering me on, and supporting me, I feel like I can conquer anything, and research shows this is true for everyone. Couples who think highly of their spouse have stronger marriages, which is such an obvious statement we often overlook it.

But you can't think highly of your spouse if you're not thinking about them at all. That's why I recommend finding ways to think of your spouse often, because the more you think of them, the more your affection toward them will grow. And guess what? Your phone can help!

If telling your partner about your love for them is not something you can rely on yourself to remember to do every day, help yourself by setting a reminder notification (yes, on your phone). Save a note from your wife and place it on your car's dashboard, so you'll see it every time you drive to work. Put a picture of you and your spouse on the lock screen of your phone. Big gestures are important, but the little things

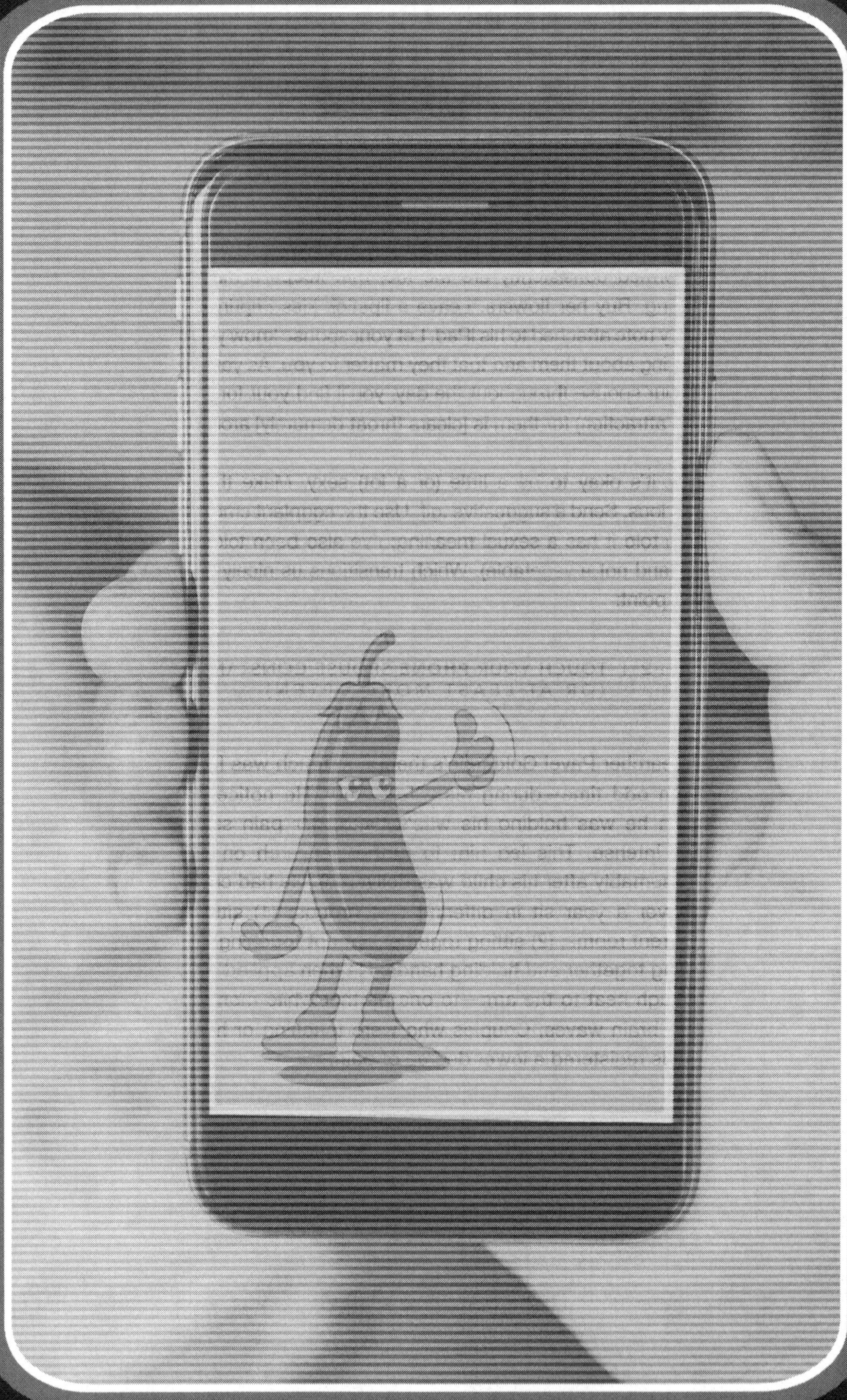

performed consistently are the fuel that keeps a marriage moving. Buy her flowers. Leave a lipstick kiss imprint on a sticky note attached to his iPad. Let your spouse know you are thinking about them and that they matter to you. As you think of your spouse throughout the day, you'll find your fondness (and attraction) for them is [clears throat demurely] aroused.

Also, it's okay to be a little (or a lot) sexy. Make the text flirtatious. Send a suggestive .gif. Use the eggplant emoji (I've been told it has a sexual meaning; I've also been told it's a fruit and not a vegetable). Which transitions us nicely to our next point:

No. 2 | TOUCH YOUR ~~PHONE~~ SPOUSE CONSTANTLY (OR AT LEAST MORE OFTEN)

Researcher Pavel Goldstein's theory on touch was formed at an odd time—during his wife's labor. He noticed that when he was holding his wife's hand, her pain seemed less intense. This led him to further research on touch (presumably after his child was delivered). He had couples of over a year sit in differing test groups: (1) sitting in different rooms; (2) sitting together but not touching; or (3) sitting together and holding hands. He then applied pain— through heat to the arm—to one partner while monitoring their brain waves. Couples who were touching or holding hands registered a lower degree of pain.

Bottom line: couples who touch one another are stronger—and able to endure more.

It makes sense that we find comfort and connection from holding hands, hugging, and kissing. Touch is a deeply physiologically ingrained human need. According to family therapist Virginia Satir, "We need four hugs a day for survival. We need eight hugs a day for maintenance. We need twelve hugs a day for growth." Now that may seem like a lot of affection, but it just shows how wired we are for touch!

Touch is good, and the more the better!

No. 3 | TAKE YOUR ~~PHONE~~ SPOUSE TO PRIVATE LOCATIONS

This one could get weird quickly if you create a connection between the bathroom and phone use. Think instead about time away, just the two of you. No kids. Not out with friends. Not staring at your phones. Just you connecting as a couple.

This doesn't have to be elaborate. I'm not suggesting doing something fancy. Take an evening stroll, grab dinner at any restaurant that doesn't have the sound of screaming kids in it—basically just take advantage of anything that creates an opportunity to connect.

Do this on a weekly basis and you'll be shocked at how close you feel. Just 1 percent of your weekly time (that's 100 minutes) will make a huge difference in your marriage. I'm a big believer that a consistent, weekly date will form a firm foundation for a healthy marriage. Everywhere I speak I hear the same excuses from couples about why they don't date now that they're married, and none of them are stronger than the reasons for why they should date. Author and researcher Shaunti Feldhahn says that couples who hang out at least once a week are five times more likely to be happy than those who don't. Being together in private doesn't need to cost a lot. It only needs to be intentional. Your calendar reveals your priorities (more on this in a moment).

No. 4 | KEEP YOUR ~~PHONE~~ SPOUSE CHARGED AND TURNED ON

Enough foreplay language already ... we're talking about sex now! Sex is an important way to bond with your spouse. It helps you feel known and loved while building trust and connection. Healthy marriages make physical intimacy an indispensable part of their union. The chemicals your body produces during sex help you feel bonded and connected to your spouse. Maybe this is what the Bible is getting at when it talks about sex making us "one flesh." Sex forges a biological, psychological, emotional, and spiritual connection with our spouse that can't be recreated another way.

Regularly ask yourself, "What would turn my spouse on?" The answer might be simpler than you think. Men, it could be as easy and basic as you doing the dishes without being asked, or helping with the kids, or, well, helping anywhere. Ladies, it's even easier for you. All you have to do is wink, speak, or sometimes just breathe, depending on the mood your husband is in. Also nudity, or near nudity, or the promise of nudity, or making us think of nudity ...

If you'll excuse me, I need to text Cathy a vegetable emoji.

Pro tip:
There's a good chance you are wrong about what turns your spouse on. According to my expert research, and this will surprise you, men and women are—wait for it—different. I know. Shocking. Because we are so different, it's easy to project what we want onto our spouse. I joke about men being visual, but maybe what your husband actually needs is a back rub, or an attentive ear. Husbands, something you're doing might be a turn-off to your wife, but she's never told you because she doesn't want to hurt your feelings.

And, honestly, this is one of the greatest gifts sex gives us. It forces us to communicate to our spouses our most intimate, private, vulnerable wants and desires. So lean into that ... again and again.

Also, if you are having issues with physical intimacy, I want to tell you that (1) you're not alone, (2) it's nothing to be ashamed of, and (3) don't give up on sex. Most sexual issues in marriage aren't physical; they're emotional or relational. Regardless of the cause, trained therapists are ready to help you. It is so important to keep the sparks flying, or to reignite a fire that's fading.

No. 5 | SPEND MONEY ON YOUR ~~PHONE~~ SPOUSE

This isn't about materialism. It's about love.

In his book The Five Love Languages, Gary Chapman declares that gifts are one of the five primary ways in which people feel loved. He writes: "Gifts need not be expensive; after all, 'it's the thought that counts.' But I remind you, it is not the thought left in your head that counts; it is the gift that came out of the thought that communicates emotional love."

There's something powerful about giving gifts to your spouse. Gifts are not about the money you spend. They are about the statement you make. And usually the statement is, "I was thinking of you."

My wife loves gifts! It's not because she's materialistic, but because gifts communicate "I missed being with you. I'm better when you are by my side." Cathy's favorite candy is Whoppers—super inexpensive, right? But when I pair them with a thoughtful, handwritten card, it's priceless to her.

I hope you can envision yourself taking these actions with your spouse. They're not new actions nor complex, but they do require intentionality and effort.

We're heading into the final stretch of the book, but before you finish, take some time to think through how these seven actions might make their way into your marriage. Be as specific as possible and share your answers with your spouse.

No. 6 | GIVE YOUR ~~PHONE~~ SPOUSE ATTENTION FIRST THING IN THE MORNING

If you and your spouse don't have a connecting routine first thing in the morning, consider developing one. Marriage experts point to the power of connecting rituals like enjoying coffee, saying a prayer over breakfast, or simply giving one another a hug and kiss to start the day. Find something within your morning routine that says, "I see you and love you." Connecting rituals aren't breakfast in bed or morning sex (as great as those can be), but sustainable, daily routines. The Bible says God's mercies are "new every morning," and that's not a bad template for our marriages. Find something you can

WAKE UP

do every morning that renews your vow to your spouse, that says "I still love you."

Cathy and I joke that our morning routine consists of one simple ritual: avoidance. Now, before you call me a hypocrite, hear me out. Cathy and I are not morning people. If you bought me that alarm clock that simulates sunrise, I would assume you hated me. Since we're not morning people, we don't place unreasonable expectations on ourselves. We have an understanding that only two actions are expected of us: (1) a good-morning hug, and (2) a goodbye kiss. This allows us to communicate that we love each other through clear, repeatable (and brief) actions. It also means we're not trying to be our very best during the time of day where we are silently rattling off curse words at the sun.

It works for us—it's our morning ritual.
Find what works for you!

No. 7 | MAKE MEMORIES WITH YOUR ~~PHONE~~ SPOUSE

This one is a lot of fun but requires some planning. We like to think of love as being spontaneous, when in reality love is intentional. The things we love are the things we intentionally give thought and effort to.

71

This is why a weekly date is such a big deal. Yes, I know I already mentioned this, but each week is an opportunity for you to make a memory. These dates don't have to be mind-blowingly creative or spectacular to nourish your relationship. Honestly, you won't remember most of them, but there will be moments that catch you by surprise and become cherished shared memories.

This also means being thoughtful about the special moments. Don't mail in your next anniversary. Start talking with your spouse now about celebrating your next big holiday in a meaningful way. Start saving now for a dream vacation in five years. Create a marriage "bucket list" and calendar out when you'll do them.

No. 8 | MAKE MEMORIES WITH YOUR ~~PHONE~~ SPOUSE

This one is a lot of fun but requires some planning. We like to think of love as being spontaneous, when in reality love is intentional. The things we love are the things we intentionally give thought and effort to.

This is why a weekly date is such a big deal. Yes, I know I already mentioned this, but each week is an opportunity for you to make a memory. These dates don't have to be mind-blowingly creative or spectacular to nourish your relationship. Honestly, you won't remember most of them, but there will be moments that catch you by surprise and become cherished shared memories.

73

C H A P T E R   S I X

If you really think about it, this whole book is about the power of presence. Your undistracted, daily attention to your spouse communicates, "I love you more than I love my phone."

Presence means I put my phone down and lift my head up. It means I make eye contact. I smile. I ask meaningful questions. I show interest in what is going on in the life of the person I am with. I must allow my heart to feel the very real needs of the person across from me. All this says, "You matter to me. I am with you."

Accomplishing this won't come easily, unfortunately. You will have to be brutally honest about your phone use. It'll mean putting your spouse's needs above your own. And it will be a choice you make every day.

It's sad, but we allow our phones to rob us of the power of presence far too often. When I am with people and their phone is constantly buzzing from texts or notifications, it's super distracting. I'm tempted to grab their face and say, "My eyes are up here!"

If I check my phone while someone is talking to me, it communicates that "this is more important than you." That might sound harsh—it might not be our intention—but it's true. You can't multitask or shortcut relationships. When your phone is omnipresent, you are not being present, period. And what you focus on determines what you love.

This is why describing phone addiction as an affair isn't as crazy as it sounds. No, you're not engaging in a sex act with your phone—it is not another man or woman you are choosing—but you are choosing something over your spouse. Your mobile is your mistress. This is sometimes called emotional infidelity, when you've given your affections to someone or something other than your spouse.

We all have to ask this uncomfortable question in our marriage:

"At what point am I choosing to spend more time with my phone than I am with my spouse?" Answering this question honestly can open your heart to the marriage you were meant to have.

C H A P T E R S E V E N

The good news is that while you can't change your marriage all at once, you can make changes that will transform you and your spouse's relationship over time. Here are some small changes that add up to big results.

No. 1 | IDENTIFY YOUR RELATIONAL VALUES

Have you ever thought about what type of spouse, parent, child, friend, or neighbor you want to be?

I would encourage you to set aside time to list your core relational values. It doesn't have to be elaborate, just a list of characteristics you want to have in your relationships. On one side of the page, write down what your current values are based on how you're spending your time, energy, and resources. Be honest. On the other side, write what you would like your relational values to be. Finally, list what is currently distracting you from developing these relational values. The time you spend on this exercise may be life-altering for you and those around you.

When these new relational values become convictions, it will no longer make sense to spend 4+ hours (the adult daily average) on your phone while spending just a few minutes with your spouse. You may discover you've been busy connecting to the entire world through your phone, while your entire world (your spouse) is right in front of you, waiting for a deeper connection.

No. 2 | EVALUATE YOUR OWN PHONE USAGE

This is all about asking why. As in, why do you reach for your phone? More specifically, why do you engage in the never-ending phone loop ritual of checking your email, Instagram, Twitter, Snapchat, and then email again? It's like circling an airport waiting to pick someone up, driving around, and around, and around, wasting time, waiting for something to happen.

But there's always something happening in our inner worlds—thoughts, fears, dreams, grudges, memories—and many times these feelings are on-ramps to understanding the truest parts of us. Phones are often ways to avoid stillness, reflection, and thinking, but they don't have to be. Start by identifying the apps essential to your daily life and then delete those that aren't. Err on the side of deleting too many—you can always reinstall them later.

Another good discipline is to identify a few waiting activities that free you from the "social media airport loop." When you're waiting at a red light or standing in line, don't drop your head to your screen. Instead, think, dream, pray, invent, talk to a stranger, or (I know this will sound radical) carry an actual book with you. Even the hipsters* will be impressed with how retro* you are.

*Are the kids still saying "hipster" and "retro" these days? I just felt you roll your eyes at me.

85

No. 3 | CREATE AND KEEP BOUNDARIES

If you discover you've got an unhealthy relationship with your phone, it's both wise and timely to establish some phone boundaries. I'm not going to create the boundaries for you, but here are four places that seem to be the most troublesome in marriage:

- when going to bed
- when sitting down for a meal
- while driving in your car together
- while participating in leisure activities

All four of these places are an on-ramp for husband/wife connection. Yes, even while driving! My wife learned early in our marriage that I actually like talking in the car because I don't have to make constant eye contact. I thought I was the only one like this, but when I started confessing it at speaking events, men laughed because they identified. Don't rob yourself of this prime opportunity for connection by looking at your phone when your spouse is driving. Be a captive audience.

It's worth creating a few mutually agreed upon boundaries. Here are some simple, non-combative ways to start the conversation:

"Can we talk about our phone use when we're together?" The emphasis is on the word "our" as this is typically a "two of us" issue.

"When you're on your phone [in bed, at the table, in the car, etc.], I feel..." Focus on expressing what you feel without accusing. Remember, it's likely that the hurt caused by your spouse's phone use is totally unintentional.

"Could we try 'experimenting' with some phone boundaries?" Describing it as an "experiment" lessens the chance of conflict. You're not saying "this is an ultimatum for all of eternity." Experiments are, by definition, revisited. It communicates humility and a willingness to be flexible, which is priceless in a marriage.

No. 4 | POWER DOWN REGULARLY

Did you know your phone has an off button? It's true! There is one! Consult your phone's manual for more information.

Learning to power-down your phone is a powerful practice. It is a reminder that your phone is not your master and that you can set it down when you choose. The truth is—and I have confirmed this via medical science and scholarly journals—you will continue to live even when your phone is off. Actually, the more you power down, the more alive you might feel.

The American Psychological Association's Stress in America report stated, "Three-quarters of American adults agree that periodically unplugging or taking a 'digital detox' would be good for their mental health.

Yet less than a quarter have actually done so." This would be laughable if it wasn't so relatable. (And sad.) We know it would be good for us to place better boundaries around our phone use, but we don't. Consider being a part of the 25 percent who are scheduling time each day to power down.

No. 5 | SET UP "SPEEDBUMPS"

A speedbump on a road is a small obstacle that should—in theory—slow you down. What would it look like for you to set up "speedbumps" that slow you down when you reach for your phone?

A friend of mine has a little miniature jail cell that he puts the family phones in when he and his family are sitting down for a meal. It is a simple speedbump that reminds everyone that meals are a great opportunity to connect.

For me, a speedbump is necessary between the impulse (wanting to distract myself on my phone) and the action (grabbing my phone and missing out on the moment). I need something to stop me when I'm itching for that "techno-fix" or when someone is sending me a text that I must look at or I'll literally explode.* To help me, I created a sticker for the back of my phone to serve as a speedbump.

*Figuratively, actually.

This simple sticker* contains a picture of a bumble bee and a wrapped present, reminding me to BeePresent. I realize this could be confused to mean "Bumble Gift" or "Stinger Package" or "Buzz Box," but it's my sticker and not yours, and I know what it means, so back off. It reminds me that being present with whomever I'm with is more important than the unknown trying to grab my attention. When I'm with people I want to be with them, so I put my phone upside down so the sticker reminds me of this relational value and slows me down from picking up my phone and phubbing others.

*You can find these stickers at:
BeePresentWeb.WixSite.com/stickers

C H A P T E R   E I G H T

My hope is this little book helps you find a new level of freedom when it comes to your phone—and a new level of connection when it comes to your marriage.

The "new normal," where couples sit together in silence while they're consumed with their phone, has to be addressed, and while I don't have all the solutions for this problem, I'm willing to engage in the conversation and call it what it is: a relational disconnection. We are better than this! Our spouses deserve more from us than a warm body with a detached mind, drifting through the vastness of the internet. Presence matters, and I hope these thoughts inspire you to reflect and make changes.

Remember, like any change worth making, it will take time and practice. A battle like this is never easy for any of us, including me! So give yourself and your spouse grace as you disconnect from your phones and reconnect with each other.

I believe in you. You can do this! And when you do, you'll discover a level of connection with your spouse you didn't know was possible.

APPENDIX

1. Practice finishing a conversation without looking at your incoming text(s). In addition, try conditioning yourself (when you're by yourself) to not look at your incoming texts immediately. You're in control of your time—others don't always need to jump into your world (via text) and ambush your time.

2. Try to determine the "why" behind always picking up your phone. Are you trying to escape something? Are you feeling the need to be validated by a post or a tweet or a picture? Are you bored? What's the "why?" behind your action? Most likely, something is driving you to this distraction, and you might as well know what it is so you can attempt to heal/fix/change it.

3. Put a photo of people who are most important to you on your phone homepage so when you reach for your phone you'll be reminded who matters most.

4. Identify your "looping" movements (i.e. I check email, then Twitter, then Instagram, then Facebook, then Snapchat, then I repeat the loop...). These habitual loops kick open the door of wasted time.

5. Make a list of things you'd really like to do if you had more time. Review the list daily and think about these actions. Get excited about accomplishing them if you had the time. Add to this list regularly. Begin to take note of how often you get distracted for 30 minutes looking at your social media apps instead of doing what you really want to do.

6. Move your most time-robbing apps off your phone's front page—or delete them. You can always reinstall them if you miss them too much. Put your apps in folders so they're not as noticeable on your phone (delete some along the way). When they're not as visible, you'll be less tempted to scroll through them mindlessly.

7. Disable all notifications, so that everything happening behind the scenes doesn't end up on your home page. If you don't know how, Google "disable notifications" or ask an 11 year old to do it for you.

8. Put a BeePresent™ sticker or some other "speedbump" reminder on the back of your phone. If you must have your phone out during a meeting, turn it upside down to be reminded to be present.

9. Assign times for a digital Sabbath/rest/fast (whatever you want to call it). Separate from your phone daily, weekly, monthly. Increase the time you allocate for this separation until you get to a point where you actually look forward to being untethered.

10. Buy a jail cell for your phone(s). Put it on the kitchen table or in any phone-free zone in your house. You can set the timer/lock for up to 60 minutes, and during that time no one can access their phone. **Go to Amazon and search "phone jail."**

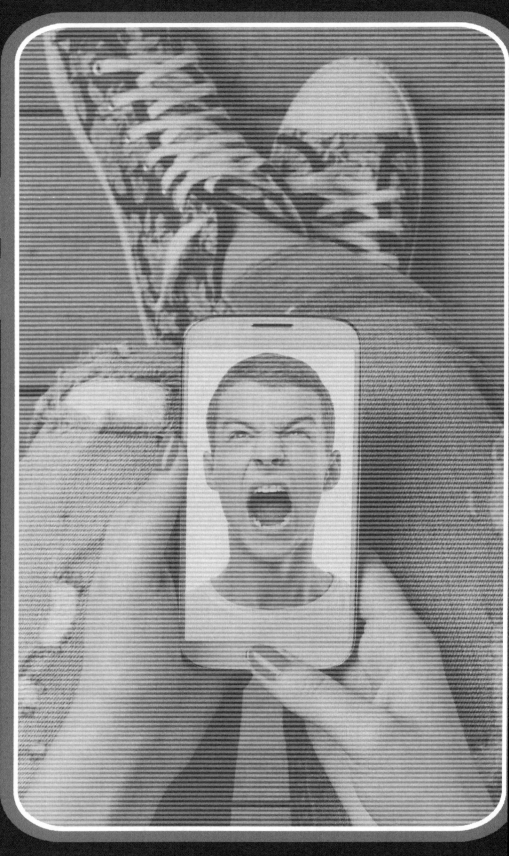

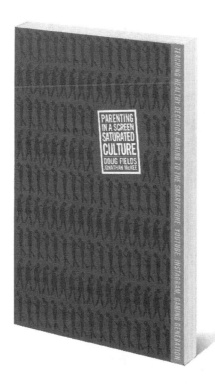

Doug's Opinion: If you're a parent, I think it's borderline crazy to give your kids a phone without some sort of contract—about use and misuse. This will sound wild, but I think it's potentially more dangerous to a young person than a car. If you need help with this, I've written a workbook called Parenting in a Screen Saturated Culture: Teaching healthy decision-making to the smartphone, YouTube, Instagram, gaming generation. Please, if it's not my book, find another resource to help you BEFORE you give your child a phone.

Doug Fields is a speaker, consultant and author of more than 50 books, including 7 Ways To Be Her Hero—The one your wife has been waiting for; Getting Ready for Marriage; and Your First Few Years of Marriage. He and his wife, Cathy, live in Southern California near his three married children. More information is available at dougfields.com.

Made in the
USA
Lexington, KY